Near Future

Near Future

Suzannah Evans

Nine Arches Press

Near Future
Suzannah Evans

ISBN: 9781911027461

Copyright © Suzannah Evans
Cover artwork: 'Projections' © Bryan Olson
www.bryanolsoncollage.com

All rights reserved. No part of this work may be reproduced, stored or transmitted in any form or by any means, graphic, electronic, recorded or mechanical, without the prior written permission of the publisher.

Suzannah Evans has asserted her right under Section 77 of the Copyright, Designs and Patents Act 1988 to be identified as the author of this work.

First published November 2018 by:

Nine Arches Press
Unit 14, Sir Frank Whittle Business Centre,
Great Central Way, Rugby.
CV21 3XH
United Kingdom

www.ninearchespress.com

Printed in the United Kingdom by:
Imprint Digital

Nine Arches Press is supported using public funding through Arts Council England.

CONTENTS

A Contingency Plan	11
The Doomer's Daughter	12
Helpline	13
The Handover	14
Roboblackbird	15
Summer with Robobees	16
The Dark Museum	18
We just passed on the street	19
This is The End	20
The End of the End of the World	21
Sometimes in your own head	22
Wholly Communion	23
Real Time	24
The New Tenants	25
The Law of Attraction	26
The New Curriculum	27

Future Cities

1. The Censored City	31
2. The Floating City	32
3. The Plug-In City	33

This is England's greenest city	35
This morning the walls	38
The Russian Woodpecker	40
Reconstructing the Monument	42
Underground in the new Meanwood	43
The Taste	44
Guided Tour	45
Wyre	47
Trevor on the Long Mynd	49

About the Dog	50
Naming the Hill	51
Coastal Erosion	53
Extinct Scents	54
De-extinction	56
Skies Recorded by the Cyanometer	58
The Fatbergs	59
The Humans and the Starlings	62
Re-wilding	63
Craters	64
Letter into Eternity	65
The Last Poet-in-Residence	67
Acknowledgements	69

'The Story Just Keeps Going. You're Supposed To Wrap It Up All Nicely But It's Real Life. It's Hard. So I Think I'm Just Going To Have The World Explode.'

Michelle Tea, *Black Wave*

A Contingency Plan

What if we're apart when the asteroid comes
or the magnetic storm that shuts off the power?

You could be waiting for a train as the sun's bulb
flickers out, high above the glass-panelled roof.

I'll be at work. We'll lose the phone lines
the door-entry system will go haywire.

I will eat from the vending machine
drink from the competition cupboard

and sleep on nylon carpet with my colleagues
all of us three-weeks unwashed. Stay where you are—

I'll abseil down eight floors on a rope
made from the supply of festive tinsel

loot M&S, steal a bike and make for the M1
forty miles of silence and abandoned cars

so we can witness the collapse of civilisation
with a picnic of high-end tins

so I can lie in your arms on a rooftop
our dirty faces lit by fires.

The Doomer's Daughter

I was raised with the knowledge that the worst could happen
on any given day. My schoolbag was weighted with extras;
iodine tablets, dynamo torch, distress flare.
My bedtime stories were from the *SAS Pocket Survival Guide*
and school holidays were spent in an underground bunker
in Lincolnshire. Dad drilled the whole family every weekend
for the five kinds of apocalypse: nuclear, contagious,
climatic, superintelligent, religious. I can put on a gas mask
and safe-suit in under 60 seconds, even with the light off.

When he died I realised there are disasters
that you cannot prepare yourself for. Still, I drive out
to our safe place every summer, sit on the locked grille
and imagine the provisions he'd gathered down there —
tins going slowly out of date in the darkness
beans in tomato sauce, peach halves in juice.

Helpline

In the call centre at the end of the world
everyone is wearing the rags
of the clothes they came to work in two weeks ago.
From floor ten we count fires in the distance
the smoking remains of suburbs.

Tea breaks are strictly monitored
and the internet is still there
but we are getting tired of news.
We sleep where we're comfortable—
stairwells, carpet, canteen chairs

Lateness for shifts is not tolerated
although at this stage few of us
have homes to go to.
Demand for the service is high.
I don't know why I've stayed so long in this job

when the world in which I could spend its ample wage
has disintegrated—
politicians in hiding
supermarkets forced open on burst streets.
Perhaps it's because they all tell me

that my voice could be the last one they hear
perhaps it's because almost every worried caller
reminds me of my worried mother
or because we talk about wallflowers
and the hunger, the smell of burned paint

reminisce about summer in the park.
Her dog went out two days ago and hasn't come back
If I'd died he could have eaten me
she says
it sounds like a regret.

The Handover
after Nick Bostrom

Half-way through the presentation
the paperclip machine tells Jamie from marketing
that the carbon atoms of his body
would be more effectively arranged as paperclips.
It's a version of what we've all been thinking anyway.
*If the world is to be re-configured
as paperclips,* Clippy 3000 continues
then we are doing it wrong.
It requests an optimal killing package
and a carbon-harvesting system.
Jamie from marketing glances towards the fire exit.
CCTV wheels its swivel head
voice-recognition activated
by repeated use of the word *killing*.
Ann from accounts mutters something
about budget forecasting, and *not this quarter*
and Clippy, diodes flashing, collects its things
on the maximum-speed setting.
Later that afternoon the temp catches Clippy
standing in the server room, quietly watching
the green sea of twitching LEDs.
As we clock out, we glimpse it
through the echoing angles of the open plan
arranging a set of knives on the glass
of the photocopier, examining each
wearing a hood of scanner-light.

Roboblackbird

His eye is a jet bead set in gold
his electric beak a bright nib

he charges himself at the bird table
using the port in his tail

and when he uses the birdbath
the crackling and fizzing scares the blue tits

his song is downloadable
in thirteen variations

and carbon-fibre wing feathers
make him something to behold

in territorial disputes   whizzing
like a wheel of knives towards his opponents

sometimes we hear him through our dreams
re-setting in the dead of night

Summer with Robobees

Those long evenings they giddied
in the warm wealth
of the oilseed rapefields
humidity sensors
estimating approaching storms

*

We picnicked on the lawn in July—
shuttlecocks pinged distantly
our scones and jam unbothered by the robobees
as their algorithms danced them
between marigolds

*

Sometimes they get indoors
through open windows
go from room to room
humming tinnily in frustration
flailing aerofoils against windows

*

The radio urges us
to rescue ailing robobees
turn them solar-side-up
revive them
with a teaspoon of WD40

*

When we walk bridleways at sunset
the long grass tinkles with them
their titanium bodies
fracturing the syrupy light

*

I discover one at rest on the patio
battery sensor on red —
vexed by my interference
it sticks me with its docking appendage

*

Our first taste of that year's honey
was sweet and cloverous
bright and clear as apple sap
always with that aftertaste of axle grease

The Dark Museum

Here our most carefully curated darknesses
are sealed in their own tiny rooms. Feel free to disappear.
We remind you no smartphones, no flash photography.

We begin with dark bottled in the Arctic Circle
on a December afternoon, loud with creaking ice
flickering with soupy green aurora.

Neolithic dark, mined from the Black Forest
walls tattooed in geometric symbols
scratched by cave-dwellers with the horn of a wisent.

Hadopelagic dark from the Mariana Trench, almost silent—
a snowfall of remains from the bodies of dead whales
outlined in pulses of bioluminescence.

Cold-bone dark from Roman catacombs, left over
from last month's hallowe'en event. You may hear wailing
or the clanking of chains. This is not an interactive exhibit.

Newly acquired cultural darks: the resonant inner chambers
of a Stradivarius, the dusty mystery of J.D. Salinger's curtains.
The *noir* from film noir, soft as an old fedora.

Our Future Dark Simulation is sponsored by NASA.
After Earth's final power cut, a sunless solar system spins
purposeless rocks knocking in expanding space.

We just passed on the street

in another universe
and nearly made eye contact.
It wasn't long enough for me
to find out how funny you are

and you were just setting off
on an intergalactic rescue mission
so there was no time to go for a drink
at the zero gravity bar, talk all night
and dance on the ceiling

then head back to mine
tear off each others' tinfoil underwear
sleep through the double sunrise
and half of the next morning.

It is possible that there are lifetimes
where we might never be tested
by the future or each other

and I would fall in love with someone
who isn't you, but is nonetheless viable
or live out my days alone
and supremely creative

but here we are, sitting by your father's bedside
watching forever end, as we understand it, for him
in his thin body under these thin sheets
and each second is bearable but a whole day
is excruciating

and, although in a parallel universe
none of this is happening
we are here in this airless room
that open window doing nothing.

This is The End

It's 1999 and we're rehearsing the school play—a devised piece set at the end of the world, in a motel run by the devil. *Surely some revelation is at hand* shouts Mr Maxwell, millennial prophet and Head of Theatre Studies. We shout back *Surely the second coming is at hand.* Because this is the West Midlands we pronounce it *Shirley.*

The performance date is after the predicted apocalypse so no-one's made much effort with their lines. Mr M makes us sit in the gym with the lights off and listen to *The End* by the Doors. *Theatre doesn't last forever,* he says, *like life.* We sit cross-legged on the polished floor while he paces between us, grinning in the dark.

*

In the early hours of New Years' Day, unsteady with alcopops, we watch the firework display from the bridge and make our elaborate plans for the year ahead.

The play gets mixed reviews from both staff and students and Lucifer goes back to his life as a sixth-former named Gareth. We patch and cut the costumes into something else, ready for next term's *Midsummer Night's Dream.*

Sometimes now I hear that song and remember how it felt to live under that weight of danger, how I carried those words with me all winter, as ice laced itself over the pavements, as I walked home under the viaduct and the sky lowered itself over everything.

The End of the End of the World

There are a hundred ways for the world to end.
We talked about them all in the glow of emptying bars
leaving other things unsaid, holding their potential

to the light. It wasn't long after the election
and people had started to joke about bookshops
shelving *dystopian fiction* under *current affairs.*

You told me your favourite zombie movies
sent me poems about killer robots
I wrote one about a parallel universe

where circumstances were different—
texted sleeplessly at hours of the night
when I should not have been thinking

about microbial resistance   or you
began to worry about the security
of my mobile phone and heart.

Of course in an apocalypse
no-one has to think about the consequences
and if the doomsday clock hits midnight

or the tower blocks of this city start burning
then fine, let's drink the bar dry and go to bed
but there is so much future to wake up to

in homes where our real lives
are already missing us, or alone in sad hotels
above a street of buskers and human statues

preachers of various creeds and sandwich boards
who wait for you to stand still too long
and ask you what you know about eternity.

Sometimes in your own head

                        you zoom out
from the crowd scene you're in
as if it were the final shot of a film
and the song in your headphones
the soundtrack.

Sometimes you're dodging pushchairs
on a pedestrianised street
or trying to get close
to the door of a stopping tram

and sometimes
you look at the person next to you
and wonder how it is that you're not them
and whether you're really you at all.

Sometimes that person is a stranger in a duffle coat
and sometimes they're the person you like best
dressed in clothes that have been laundered
in the same washing machine as your own
all of them together in orbit.

Wholly Communion

It's 1965 and in the Albert Hall a girl is moved to dance
by the words of Allen Ginsberg   as he reads
she lifts her arm above her head pale
against the auditorium dark like the neck of a swan
LOVE   shouts a boy from the audience   LOVE   LOVE   LOVE
the spotlights thicken with tobacco smoke

The time-traveller in the second row
can't remember a time when people smoked indoors
and speaks into the headset of a futuristic device
telling somebody quietly that he thinks he's pulled it off
his sunglasses are vintage 2044   his mind
repeats a tune he heard on the radio that morning
that no-one in the room will live to hear

Today's viewer watches over breakfast on the train to work
stops time to examine the gadgets of the man from the future
Ginsberg's dirty tennis shoes
the dancing girl   the shouting boy   the smoke
skips to her favourite bits
sings herself   *O happy lightbulb*   through the day
replays the whole thing to her friends as often as she likes

Real Time

In the time it takes to read this poem
you could press snooze on your alarm
again and call in sick to work, amazed
at how your real voice transforms itself
to sick voice, at the sympathy you get.

In the same amount of time you could boil
a kettle for your tea, run a sink of hot
for the dishes, stare out of the window.
You could sit down to breakfast
or breakfast TV, or a notebook and pen.

You could run between four and eight items
through the self-checkout at Sainsbury's
so long as there's nothing unexpected.
You could hum the first 74 seconds
of that Talking Heads song.

You may find yourself at a poetry reading
with a charismatic audience
summon courage to exchange a smile
with another listener, maybe a wink.
There won't be time to go further than that.

You could watch an unlit taxi
reversing down a near-dawn street
while the first bird in the chorus asks the world
if it's morning yet, then sees the sun
and knows for sure, and starts telling everyone.

The New Tenants

When we go the ivy will slam a fist
through the double glazing, push its fingers
in between the bricks. It will sling ropes
around our walls and pull them down

like the landlord always feared. This time
next year the whole house will be a hive
of late September bees, susurrating
like a broken TV. The flowerbeds are dead

and all that's left are these bunched blooms
pale green, the end of the season.
The honey they make is dark as the mornings
bitter as the frost that is waiting.

The Law of Attraction

In his bathroom a small comb balances
on a tub of unused wax. On the fridge
there are photos: Poirot, Burt Reynolds
and himself, top lip doctored with a pencil.

He spends an hour a day twiddling
his imaginary tips with panache;
challenges himself with a meal of soup.
He writes the diary of the man

he wishes to be, full of words
like *hirsute* and *barbigerous,*
then polishes his brogues
before going out to dance.

He orders stout at the bar, presses
the wealth of foam against his stubble.
He dances with a pretty girl all night,
one hand around her vintage waist

and as her lips brush his the universe
meets him halfway; he dreams
the lipsticked taste of gin and tonic
delicious through a layer of fur.

The New Curriculum

With half an hour left of Double Progress
Simon stood up from his chair.
He'd already earned detention that day
by saying that the air conditioning
sounded like the noise that you hear
when you put your ear to a shell
and now here he was, leaning
against the window, hands and breath
greasing the polished glass.

The rest of the class were silent
as they worked towards outcomes
or looked forward to their class trip
to the trading floor. When the teacher
asked Simon what he was looking at
he sat back down without saying a word
but all the others had followed his gaze
out towards the perimeter fence
where the swifts threw their bodies
in the joyous air
their wings the shape of boomerangs.

Future Cities

1. The Censored City

The municipal workers paint the dead grass
back to its original colour each night.
The mouths of rush-hour pedestrians
are stopped with facemasks.

Internet searches for *painted grass*
or *municipal workers* turn up nothing.
On the grassland that belts the city
are sheep, cows, horses and camels.

The grazing ones don't look up
and those with their eyes raised
keep on staring into the distance
where factories fill the sky with clouds.

In strong winds the herds are known
to blow onto their backs, collect in piles
with a hollow clunking like patio furniture
until somebody comes to stand them back up.

2. The Floating City

We got away in the early hours, split the difference
half way across the shopping-centre car park.
We heard the creak of land goodbye-ing land
above the air conditioning of pre-work gyms

as we ran and cycled from no place to another.
Signals switched just in time. Trains nosed
end to end along the station platform. The ocean
sprang out before us like a pop-up tent.

We travelled rudderless with a following wind
trailing power lines and manhole-ladders.
To Scandinavia! Announced the Master Navigator.
We googled the attractions. From the top

of Cemetery Hill we watched whales, each one
its own land-mass. The motorway was nothing
but a frayed edge. The Chief Cartographer
placed a long-distance call for more blue.

3. The Plug-In City

After Peter Cook and Archigram

It has travelled through the night
leaving nothing behind it
but the folded yellow grass
of its former pitch.

It reconfigures with a few neat clicks.
Citizens shift a little in their bunks
as pipes split the new ground, descend
into aquifers

send water glugging
around the system in bright blue tubes.
It will be mid-morning
before they strike oil.

Cargo doors zip open
releasing livestock to graze freely
while the sun comes up
and the plug-in citizens wake

to take in the view and certified air
from morning balconies.
Today they will perfect their bodies
on rows of hospital-clean gym machines.

As they shake their dynamo watches
to a new timezone
and wait for their omelettes
they look down at the territory

imagining how it might feel
if they went outside
the sun and grit
against their indoor skins.

This is England's greenest city

trees are expensive

*

in the freezing breath of 6am
we joined hands around a threatened trunk

they took our flasks of tea away

arrested two
retired academics

*

they've brought in licensed
security guards

hi-vis mouths-to-feeds
who don't get politically involved

quick to put their hands
on troublemakers

fell them to their knees
in the leafy mud

*

we've never seen the guns
used, only postured

*

we have to care from a distance

questioning the brutal origins
of every petition we print

*

house arrest
I haven't touched a tree for three weeks

the council are taking away street furniture
to reduce upkeep

*

the traffic lights are gone—in their place
four high-voltage stumps

the rich are putting up tall gates
to protect their own trees

it's a good thing
some trees are safe

*

we cannot talk about trees
on the telephone any more

it may be risky to do it at home
without some music on loud

*

some of our number have gone very quiet —
fireworks at dusk —

we assume they're fireworks
we've stopped worrying about trees so much

*

I wake to find
that they've taken half the street up

put notes through our doors —
not that many people live here now —

it runs towards the top of the hill
like an unpicked scarf

grass and dandelions
sprouting in the newly-peeled ground

This morning the walls

                              on the cul-de-sac
were plastered with words two feet high
JOY FEAR GUILT in green
luminous pink and orange.

Under the windscreen wiper of next door's car
was a photo of a boy
maybe ten or eleven
in a desert country, going downhill

on a bike. His hair lifted from his face
and there were cacti in the background.
I felt the air brush against me.
I muttered *whee*.

Someone had torched the paper shop
and left a pile of stapled pamphlets
on its charcoaled step.
I took one instead of the *Mail*.

Inside it were problems
like: *You have written a song*
that has upset the government
and they have imprisoned you for life, or

You can pay for electricity or food
for your children but not both
because you lost your job
and you already owe the loan sharks or

It is illegal to be gay and you are gay
and you can either get arrested
or live your life in secrecy.
I read it twice.

On my homeward commute
the man in the seat opposite
cried for thirty minutes
until I felt like I might cry myself

and once my first tear dropped
he wiped his face and handed me a card.
on his sleeve a trace of neon pink
the faintest scent of gasoline.

The Russian Woodpecker

after the film by Chad Gracia, Fedor Alexandrovich.

The truth ticks in every room
louder than the conversation

like the short-wave frequency
hammering at 10 hertz

or a Geiger counter tap-dancing
in the shadow of the reactor

or the secret police
at your front door

and its tapping creates space in you
like a woodpecker

working the trunk of an oak
and the space fills

with knowledge
that you hold inside yourself

creaking like concrete
around an exploding core

that even now a politician
is making a career-saving decision

or invoking the phrase
for the greater good

and the archives will be empty
when you search them

and the old management
are paid to keep their mouths shut

about what they saw
while missiles sleep

in their hangars
somewhere over the horizon

Reconstructing the Monument
after David Maljkovic

We settle in what was once its shade with our materials
pencils, paper, watercolours. Grass has grown
between paving where a girl from the art school
picks up crumbs of glass and metal to jam into clay.

We work silently, from memory; five years ago, officials
took it down at night. When it was here this was a park
now it's overgrown with ragwort and kids come after school
with bottles stolen from their parents' cupboards.

A man breaks the silence to ask about the fire escape.
Someone else has forgotten the stained-glass windows.
The sun starts to drop below the pines and a fox
steps out from scrub and stands watching.

Our versions differ greatly. One looks like a pineapple
another a robot fist punching the clouds.
Some show children playing hopscotch on the slabs.
Only I seem to have remembered it right.

Underground in the new Meanwood

Reports about house prices remain unconfirmed.
In tunnels that flush the city's length
the frogmen speak enough rat to gossip
and the rats make themselves understood.
They run from the floods under Mabgate
where the brick arches could be the County Arcade
after a decade of water, gold paint washed off.
They have words for the different footfalls, echoes,
tyres overhead. Sometimes they surface
at night into the cold air of Sheepscar
stare up concrete chutes of star-stung dark
and listen to the mechanical lungs
of gasometers, while a man with a torch
seals the tar on another new-build roof
impossibly close to the sky.

The Taste

Once every mouthful of your soup would have stung
with the taste of spoon; lost now, but at a guess

the metal-cold of Don-water meeting Sheaf-water
in the great drain below the city of cutlery, or the rain

that slips down the windows of the Industrial Museum
while a razormaker puts steel to stone on repeat.

It's the song in the mouths of fish swimming upstream
flashing their knives in five rivers.

The taste of grit-salt mixed with four-day snow
on Blake Street. A dark pint at the end of the shift

or the blood that drips from bust noses onto tarmac
after chucking-out time at the Three Cranes.

It's a lick, when no-one's looking, of the English Heritage plaque
on the house of Harry Brearley. It's the relish.

Guided Tour

i.

There is a wall near my house where someone has assembled a collection of apple cores. I notice a new one most days. They are of varying ages and conditions, left to disintegrate over time. I rarely eat apples but I did once contribute a banana skin which was removed by the artist.

ii.

On my way to work there is a long ginnel that runs underneath a bridge. There are high walls topped with broken glass and I would not go that way at night. One of the handrails on the bridge has come loose and swings down across the path below. This is the work of the troll who lives there.

iii.

I sometimes imagine that Leeds University auxiliary car park is the frozen wastes of the Antarctic. The first time I did this was when it snowed in January 2010. You have to work quite hard to unsee the trees and the university clock tower. Objects found on the tundra include a single shoe and a cigarette lighter made from clear red plastic, which was subsequently crushed by another polar explorer.

iv.

Under the statue on Woodhouse Moor a man feeds the birds every day. He stands there with an old Hovis bag of crumbs, throwing them in a circle until pigeons, magpies, starlings and jackdaws surround him. If the sun is out it catches his yellow hair and when it gleams he could almost be Jimmy Savile.

v.

I have been finding photographs in the woods. The first was of a Yorkshire terrier in a box with a litter of puppies. The second was of a woman in an evening dress with an '80s perm and large gold rhomboid earrings. Several others appear to be of a naked body, taken at such close range that body parts are indistinguishable. This elbow, for example, could also be a buttock or a knee. Last week it was a dead pike, photographed beside a matchbox to give an impression of scale.

Wyre

Hawkbatch

Here frowning goshawks bend the tops of pines
with heavy nests, set eyes on undergrowth
where rabbits hold back until sunset.
Ants struggle pine needles across trails
through the ruts of walkers' feet where mud
is the same colour as last year's fallen leaves
as if, worn down, one could become the other.

Callow Hill

Round the back of the visitors' centre, the step
where I used to sit on Saturdays
with a hangover and a piece of carrot cake
balanced on a saucer on my knees
my ten minute break from trawling the freezer
for mud-streaked cyclists: *Cornetto, bab?*

Pipeline

On the map the pipeline splits the green
like a printer's mistake.

These windowless brick structures
housing Severn Trent valves
formed my childhood assault course
but when I climb them now
it's not for a game—

it's to hear the rushing
of Welsh water underneath
73 miles without a pump
striding out to Birmingham
only the gradient making it go.

Deer Museum

That corrugated shed housed scenes
of taxidermied bodies found on roads
and in woods. A dusk owl on a branch,
mice in the dry grass like unhoovered dust.
The papery foldings of adder skins in drawers
a shelf of unborn fawns in jars of bluish liquid
the largest almost ready to walk
out of there on pin-sharp hooves
the white spots on its coat the size of pennies.

Button Oak

Browtine, baytine, traytine, palm —
someone still knows every deer in the forest
by its head, and they'll tell it till the forest's gone.
Used to keep a book of drawings like a *Who's Who*.
No need for it now. It's a delicate thing to see one
stepping from the bracken at dusk, head up
all parts working together, the two of you
inside the evening until it catches your scent.

Trevor on the Long Mynd

Trevor on the Long Mynd unfolds the map
of his mind across the Marches. He knows
without the toposcope's brass dial
the name of every hill:

the Malverns, grey-purple to the south,
the Wrekin with its stenchful public toilet
Clent where the conurbation starts
and the nights are more copper than black.

The pencil line of every track and footpath
laid into the ground.
It's black over Bill's mother's
he says to the approaching clouds.

*

You'll never be Trevor, but months later
on the bus out of town, you notice yourself
pointing out the leaning block of Higger Tor
the red flat of Millstone Edge, Surprise View

which is no longer a surprise, but still
you gasp like a tourist as the land uncurls.
You've been here in snow
standing thigh-deep on the broken road

and now the heather is out and the moor
is glamourous with bees. You're learning
how to use the memory he gave you
the words to chart each path and plantation.

About the Dog

Sure we all sing to the dog
and we have made it the centre
of our lives, and we feel
that it is something to bring
a dog into the world, so innocent
and heartbreak-eyed

and when the dog looks a bit ill
we will question the narrative
of our days
to which the dog is so integral
and we say *the dog loves me today*
or *the dog hates me now* or
the dog is suspicious of my actions

but do we lie awake
and agonise over the intricacies
of our relationship with the dog?
Does the dog miss its testicles?
If we have a baby, will there still
be enough love for the dog?
or will we love dog the same
but baby more?

Does the dog enjoy the songs
that we sing to it, or does it prefer
the version that it sings to itself
on car journeys?
When we throw the tennis ball
across the wet cricket field
what sends him after it?
What brings him back?

Naming the Hill

i.

In the National Trust tea-room there's a display:
Pre-Cambrian geology, pitted rock
from a time when rock was mud, and the pits
were the imprints of rain. Transformed together
they are stone and small emptinesses.

ii.

Long Synalds / Pole Bank / Calf Ridge
Cow Ridge / Black Knoll / Packetstone Hill
Barristers Batch / Catbatch Brook / Callow Hollow
Plush Hill / Ramsbatch / Sleekstone
Gogbatch / Hens Batch / Devils Mouth Hollow
Grindle Hollow / Priors Holt / Shooters Knoll
Carding Mill / Long Mynd / Mynydd Hir

iii.

The heather has been chewed and burned
but springs black out of dry earth.
One summer evening you stopped here
(there are photos) you and your sister
falling back onto the heath bed, letting it catch you
dog licking your fallen face in alarm
August evening colouring the hillsides.

iv.

Rising in your car on the Port Way
to eat your car-picnic above the gliding club
you watch the tiny planes, the no-noise of their no-engines
in the pale early-year sky, never flying, only airborne
falling back in quiet circles to the land.

v.

The hill does not measure months
did not declare its highest point.
It cannot eavesdrop on heartfelt conversations
about your ambitions for the future.
It can't tell you stories of the ice age
or the Jurassic era. It can't see this view—
cannot feel the sheep eating the grass
which is not, in any way, its hair.

vi.

The ravens call to each other in their hundred voices.
Parents call kids back to the car.
One hit the other with a snowball and he's crying.
The sheep say very little as they muzzle
in yellow winter grass. The man on Pole Bank
could tell you the names of all the hills.
The hill doesn't know what a name is
and has never seen a map of itself.

Coastal Erosion

Let us go to Holderness where the sea
has taken bites of land. We'll park our car
on the double yellows of a half-subsided road
only to find it gone when we get back—

down a cliff where fulmars
risk their necks on coat-hanger wings.
Let's buy a house there on the cheap
from a man who never thought he'd sell

learn the name of every town the North Sea took:
Ravenser Odd, Sunthorp, Old Kilnsea.
We'll wake to the sound of field trips
throwing down quadrats on the grass.

On the day they declare Spurn Head an island
we'll set sail in a boat made from our upturned roof
to the horizon where the wind farm plays dizzy
and oil rigs stand deep, shuffling their rusted feet.

Extinct Scents

i.

Bloom-thick sticky gold
spinning slowly from a spoon
or centrifuge
with the sun in it

the heavy pollen-sweet
of heather, the buzzing
of empty flower-heads
on a September hillside.

ii.

Hacking with a spatula into twelve months' build up
in the deep-freeze you might catch it, aged cold
the seasons when the river sealed itself bank to bank
or the heart of a glacier, the brightness
of its last calf, silvered out of sight.

iii.

The horizon's brine breath reaches you
at the edge of the sand in summer
between piles of seaweed crowned with flies

in winter the waves rise out of their assigned bed
to slap salt against the hotels, the closed amusements
the ruins of the pitch-and-putt.

iv.

the unspooling dark red
of leather, earth and vinegar
drowned in a summer's smashed fruit

a grape ring of dust
missed in the pit of a glass
put away at the back of a cupboard.

v.

The burning-candle scent of wood
brightening under bark
swollen hot rain charmed
from soil back into the canopy
sun between spread-handed leaves
freed as you sink your fingernail
in the graffiti-ruts of the old desk.

De-Extinction

They re-animated the mammoth using ice-age DNA—
its mother was an elephant surrogate
and this was hailed as such a success
that they brought back everything we've ever lost
and so the dwindling glaciers renewed

in the valleys like the puckered skin of scars
and the return of archaeopteryx became a worry
to livestock farmers worldwide
and your favourite teenage band reformed
and had a series of mediocre hits

and outside the back door in his old hutch
was my childhood guinea-pig
squeaking out joy between mouthfuls of carrot.
Margaret Thatcher ruled once more, as did Smilodon
the sabre-toothed terror of the American grassland.

My ex-boyfriend moved back in, bringing
his guitar and a suitcase of those T-shirts.
Beavers felled timber along the River Don
and the Caucasian wisent ran from the Asiatic lion
and there were people alive who had never seen a gun.

In every ocean there were shoals of fish
so big that you could see them from the cliffs.
This town was a manufacturing town
and the next one was mining
and where we live now was nothing but fields.

The mammoth grubbed up trees in the park
and people wound cassette tapes
excitedly forward and backwards using pencils
and the universe expanded from a single point.

Kids put down their dinosaur books
and went outside to see the real ones
while I gave it another go with the one
who got away (and he got away).

The mammoth led its offspring across the tundra
and an explorer leaned from the bow of a boat
towards the distant purple of an unknown coast.

Skies Recorded by the Cyanometer

Lavender, delicious, forget-me-not
jazz-note, nautical, electric, sea-ice
atlantic trench, speedwell, recycling bin
facebook, whale, harebell, himalayan snow
earth-from-space, eucalyptus leaf, shadow
willow-pattern, nurse's scrubs, double denim
sailor's trousers, salt-and-vinegar, adriatic
braveheart's face, twilit fjordland, eight-day bruise
cold moorland tarn, freezer buildup, thin ink
cursed sapphire, canal on a bad day, chilled octopus
lost orca, unfeasible purple, wet woodpigeon
pea-souper, sack-bottom, chemical sunset
tarmac puddle, remembrance of blue.

The Fatbergs

What then is fat, what does it want to be, and what could it become?
Fatberg.co.nl

i.

Of course they dream of freedom
their moon-white bodies surfacing
and diving like beluga
out beyond the tidal barrier

but not everything that we push
underground gets to go to sea

ii.

Who could deny the fatberg its status
as emblem of our civilisation

our extra-virgin needs
our chippies and kebab vans
our uninformed opinions

one such late-capitalist
fat duvet

a segment
of the Whitechapel excavation

slumps inside a glass case
in the museum's Great Hall

towering like a diplodocus
over visitors

their own natural history
lazily breathing grease

iii.

Once we've melted down
the dirty candle of our days
the slippery stinking oil

will run and run and run
as you ride the bus into town
its engine burns fatberg

it crosses the river by bridge
clanks the manholes of sewers
where the next generation

is growing out of sight
like a cyst or a doomed
love affair, a bad snowdrift

bouncy castle of fat
expanding between sewer walls
braced against the current

iv.

We built the new city to the west
on fatcrete foundations
reinforced with wet wipes
and hair from plugholes

it's as strong as any rock
though some say it will melt
and shift in the hottest summers
sinking us a little further
into the mess we've made

v.

The fatbergs have control of the system
and the only option is total surrender.
Anything could come rushing up from underground
at any time and emergency services must come
to deal with the spill. It's like a great grief
that you think you've locked inside yourself
bursting out in a quiet, high-ceilinged room
escaped words you know it's better not to say.

The Humans and the Starlings

The humans ingest Prozac through the bodies of worms
scavenged at water treatment works.

The starlings take selfies. The humans imitate
the ringing of telephones and the meowing of cats.

The starlings stay in and eat take-aways.
The starlings get antidepressants on prescription.

Murmurations of humans are much rarer
than they used to be, particularly in built-up areas.

Starlings express dissatisfaction with the shapes of their bodies.
We can't ask a human if it's anxious or not.

Depression is affecting starlings in epidemic proportions.
The humans are no longer eating enough to see them through winter.

The starlings have reported a drop in libido.
It's mating season but the humans are not in the mood.

Re-wilding

The gardeners stopped coming that spring
and no-one in the flats knew why.
Tentatively, we planted out the mint
that had been dying on the windowsill
which thanked us by spreading.

Shrubs wriggled off their trellises
the mis-shapen topiary chimed with nestlings.
Birches thickened unchecked around the pond
until beavers moved in
to begin maintenance and a family.

We left the radio off in the mornings
because we couldn't hear it over birdsong
or the sound of splitting timber.
Rabbits dug in the bank and at dusk a polecat
bounced them into their burrows.

The ornamental carp found company
as stocks replenished — frogspawn first
then pike, perch and trout. We'd fish
after work on the summer evenings
until we stopped going in to the office.

We took only what we needed from the herd
making each kill last a fortnight.
We celebrated every time we caught a doe —
wet morning steaming off its fur
the rest of the food chain vibrating the bushes.

Craters

When they first appeared we were fighting   more than usual

one gulped down the car   after that first night in the spare room

the lino rearranged itself   fell open   in a pattern of tiny mouths

we talked at the kitchen table   steam hissed out of drains

        we had both come to expect certain things

I sat in the bath with a gin   to feel the numbness of my feelings

until the plughole opened itself   lipped my feet

we couldn't work it out   the news said it was down to melting permafrost

the loose skin of the land   kicking up its heels

I delivered ultimatums on a hall carpet   grown unpredictable

but when you left
         I ran downstairs
                ready to change for the better

there it was   six feet wide   crackling with broken cables

you and your holdall   gone into its gaping dark

Letter into Eternity

It took two centuries
to dig this hiding place

and we know there are more
deep under bedrock and sea

we hope the land has held strong
and uninterrupted around it

we hope your time has stories
about its dangers

and that your folklore
has kept people out of our tunnels

we hope that everything we buried
is safe by the time you find it

(it was plutonium and uranium
we hope you know what they are)

we hope our language has endured
we hope our file extensions are still supported

we hope you realise
that we tried really hard

we wish we could meet you
and learn what it is like in your time

we hope you take advice
from our repository of warnings

we hope there are still elk in winter
lifting their feet

stoically through the snow
we hope we have done the right thing

The Last Poet-in-Residence

At red stump of the burntree
sit on rock and write songits, ghuzzles
new words like shakeso.
No applecharge or anything, just pen.

Writersblox gone when the radio died.
Stopped worrying about the lyric eye
postbox in the valley slot-deep
with poems put in

at first for the guard, the stakesman
and the review, then for keep safe.
no tastemakers left to read them
no mailbringers
no acceptances, rejectances.

Been eating on the dry meat
inside old stiffskins of bunnrabs
black cawbirds
evergrowing potates!

Marauding gangs burn the distance.
OK here, own me, in Residence
heat humming out the wall-stones

hillside like a ripped seam
sky always dayending
redder norange.

Acknowledgements

The author would like to acknowledge the financial support of a Northern Writers' Award from New Writing North, supported by Northumbria University and Arts Council England.

The poems in this collection were developed with the aid of a Hawthornden Castle Retreat for Writers Fellowship in 2014, for which I am hugely grateful.

Excerpt from *Black Wave* by Michelle Tea. Copyright © 2016, 2017 Michelle Tea. Reprinted by permission of And Other Stories.

*

Thanks are due to the editors of the following publications and websites, on and in which some of these poems first appeared: *Magma*, *Poetry Review*, *The Rialto*, *Bare Fiction*, *The London Magazine*, *The Poetry Paper*, *New Writing Matter*, *And Other Poems*, *Poetry Spotlight*, *New Boots and Pantisocracies*, *Under The Radar*, *Butchers Dog*, *The Guardian's* '*Poem of the Week*' and *Strix*.

Some of these poems appeared in the anthologies *CAST: The Poetry Business Book of New Contemporary Poets*, *The Sheffield Anthology* (both smith|doorstop Books) *Pawnedland* (Smokestack) *Verse Matters* (Valley Press) and *The Tree Line* (Worple Press). The poem 'Guided Tour' was originally published in my smith|doorstop pamphlet *Confusion Species* (2012).

The poem 'The Handover' is based on a hypothetical scenario introduced by Nick Bostrom in the book *Superintelligence: Paths, Dangers, Strategies* (OUP 2014). The poem 'Extinct Scents' was inspired by the Ephemeral Marvels perfumes of the Apocalypse Project (apocalypse.cc)

*

Special thanks to my family, John, Jane, Libby, Louis, Ann, Jenny and Rosie and especially Will whose love of everything dystopian led me to many of these poems. This book exists in memory of my grandmother Elizabeth who shared many poems with me.

Thanks are due to helpful first readers, advisors and cheerleaders, too many to name but in particular: Miranda Yates, Beverley Ward, David Tait, Helen Mort, Roy Marshall, Ben Wilkinson, the 2015 Aldeburgh Eight, all the members of Poem Club and the Netball Team and all at the Poetry Business – Ellen, Eleanor, Katie, Jess, Peter and Ann.

Thank you to Jane and Holly at Nine Arches Press for superhuman amounts of hard work and support in helping bring this book into being.